180
Prayers
for a
Radiant
Faith

180 Prayers
for a Radiant Faith

Meditations *for* Women

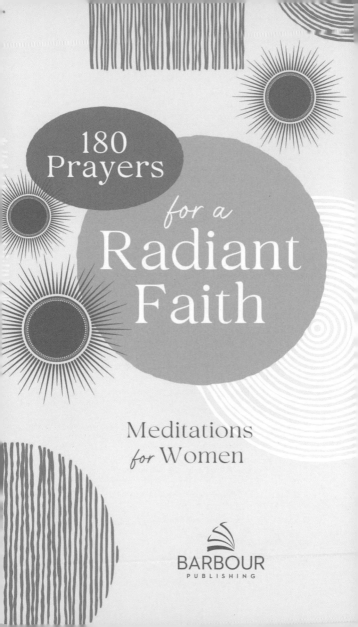

BARBOUR
PUBLISHING

You Are a Radiant Woman of God!

Now you've got my feet on the life path, all radiant from the shining of your face. Ever since you took my hand, I'm on the right way.
PSALM 16:11 MSG

The all-powerful God we serve is interested in you. In fact, He longs to hear your prayers. You are welcome—any time—to bring any petition before the King of the universe. Now that's genuine love!

The prayers in this book will help you develop a more intimate relationship with the heavenly Father. As you read the prayer selections, make them your own. Meditate on the scriptures. You may even wish to keep a journal on hand to record your personal thoughts as you reflect on God's amazing love for you.

Be blessed, radiant woman of God!

The One Who Is

Heavenly Father, today I'm grateful for all You are—the God who is, the God of the living, the great I Am. Your character is unchanging. You are the epitome of perfect holiness and love. Because of who and all You are, I believe and trust in You. Your truthfulness is indisputable and Your power is established. Not just for the majestic works by Your hand but for the pure glory of Your nature—I worship You today. Amen.

Who is like the LORD our God,
who dwells on high?
PSALM 113:5 NKJV

Grace for Everything

Father, I'm thankful for Your grace—Your unmerited favor to me through Jesus Christ, and that special strength You give Your child in times of need, trial, and temptation. If not for Your grace, I wouldn't even be able to approach You. Thank You for extending favor to me: forgiving my sins and adopting me into Your family. And thank You so much for that extra dose of perseverance that You keep giving to me in tough situations. I'm so thankful Your resource center will never experience a shortage. I praise You today for grace. Amen.

But he gives us more grace.
JAMES 4:6 NIV

Amazing Forgiveness

Lord, I come into Your presence, thanking You for forgiveness. In a culture where many experience clinical depression because of guilt, I can know my past is redeemed because of Christ's sacrifice for me. Your forgiveness is so amazing. Although I don't deserve it, You pour it out freely and lovingly. Because You have seen fit to pardon me, I bless Your name today.

In Him we have redemption through
His blood, the forgiveness of sins,
according to the riches of His grace.
EPHESIANS 1:7 NKJV

The Inspirational Word

Lord, some mornings I wake up ready to go! I feel rested and energetic. Other mornings, I wonder how I will make it through the day. Remind me that as Your child, I have a power source that is always available to me. I may not always feel joyful, but the joy of the Lord is my strength. As I spend time in Your Word, renew my strength, I pray. In Jesus' name, amen.

For the joy of the LORD is your strength.
NEHEMIAH 8:10

True Joy

Thank You, Father, for Your Word, which teaches me how to experience true joy. This world sends me a lot of messages through the media and through those who do not know You. I have tried some of the things that are supposed to bring joy, but they always leave me empty in the end. Thank You for the truth. Help me to abide in You, that I might be overflowing with joy. Amen.

These things have I spoken unto you,
that my joy might remain in you,
and that your joy might be full.

JOHN 15:11

No More Sorrow

Jesus, Your disciples were dismayed. You told them You were going away but that You would see them again. Those men had walked and talked with You. You were their leader, their friend. How lost they must have felt at Your crucifixion! But three days later. . . Wow! Lord, You turn mourning into rejoicing. Help me to trust in this. Thank You, Jesus. Amen.

And ye now therefore have sorrow: but I will see you again, and your heart shall rejoice, and your joy no man taketh from you.
JOHN 16:22

Joy in God's Word

Thank You, God, that in Your holy scriptures I find the ways of life. I find wise counsel in the pages of my Bible. You reveal the truth to me, Lord, and there is no greater blessing than to know the truth. You tell me in Your Word that the truth sets me free. I am free to live a life that brings You glory and honor. May others see the joy I have found in You! Amen.

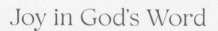

*Thou hast made known to me
the ways of life; thou shalt make me
full of joy with thy countenance.*
ACTS 2:28

Glorifying God
in My Work

God, today as I work both in my home and outside it, may my attitude glorify You. I am not of this world, but I am in it, and often it has too much influence on me. May I think twice before I grumble, Father, about the tasks set before me this day. I will choose to work for my Father, and may my countenance reflect Your love to those around me. Amen.

And whatsoever ye do, do it heartily,
as to the Lord, and not unto men; knowing
that of the Lord ye shall receive the reward of
the inheritance: for ye serve the Lord Christ.
COLOSSIANS 3:23–24

Putting God First

Father, a glance at my bank statement causes me to shudder. Where does my money go? Am I too concerned with what the world says I must possess to be cool, to fit in, to appear successful? Your Word says that I cannot serve both material wealth and You. I choose You, Lord. Be the Master of my life and of my checkbook. I need Your help with this. Amen.

No man can serve two masters: for either he will hate the one, and love the other; or else he will hold to the one, and despise the other. Ye cannot serve God and mammon.
MATTHEW 6:24

What Would Jesus Do?

Heavenly Father, sometimes I am a Sunday Christian. How I want to worship You with the rest of my week! Please help me to be mindful of You throughout the week. May Your will and Your ways permeate my thoughts and decisions. Whether I am taking care of things at home or working with others in the workplace, may I glorify You in all that I say and do. Amen.

Whether therefore ye eat, or drink, or whatsoever ye do, do all to the glory of God.
1 CORINTHIANS 10:31

A Giving Heart

Father, may I be honest? Sometimes I don't feel like serving. They keep asking if I will help with this or that at church. And there is always a collection being taken up. Can't I just focus on me? I have my own needs! But oh, the peace I feel when I lay my head on my pillow at night knowing I have loved with action, with sacrifice. Make me a giver, I ask. Amen.

Remember the words of the Lord Jesus, how he said, It is more blessed to give than to receive.
ACTS 20:35

Joyful in Hope

God, the longer I live, the more I realize that joy and hope go hand in hand. I have joy because my hope is in You. Thank You, Lord, that as Your daughter, I do not go out to face the day in hopelessness. No matter what happens, I can find joy because my hope is not in this world or in my circumstances. My hope is in the Lord. Amen.

---

*Happy is he that hath the
God of Jacob for his help, whose
hope is in the LORD his God.*
PSALM 146:5

Serve One Another

God, I have not been put on this earth to serve myself. It is not all about me. Sometimes I forget that! Service is what this life is all about, isn't it? Father, give me opportunities to show love to others today. Make every moment a "God moment." Help me to be aware of the many needs around me. Create in me a heart that loves others and puts them ahead of myself. Amen.

By love serve one another. For all the law is fulfilled in one word, even in this; Thou shalt love thy neighbour as thyself.
GALATIANS 5:13–14

Use Me, Lord

Savior, You laid down Your life for me. You died a horrible death on a cross. It was death by crucifixion, which was reserved for the worst of criminals. And You had done nothing wrong. You came into the world to save us! You gave Your very life for us. Jesus, take my life. Use me for Your kingdom's work. Only in losing my life for You will I save it. Amen.

For whosoever will save his life shall lose it;
but whosoever shall lose his life for my sake
and the gospel's, the same shall save it.
MARK 8:35

Provisions from God

God, there is no creature on earth You do not see or provide for. I'm bringing praise to You right now for the daily things You supply for me. It is through Your goodness that I have food to eat, clothes to wear, and water to drink. Help me always be thankful for what I have and not emulate the wandering Israelites who, focusing on lack, preferred to complain. Your power is awesome; thank You for generously supplying my needs each and every day. Amen.

You open Your hand and satisfy the desire of every living thing.
PSALM 145:16 NKJV

Honoring My Parents

Heavenly Father, show me how to honor my parents. Even as I have grown into a woman, Your command remains. Give me patience with my parents. Remind me that with age comes wisdom. Help me to seek their counsel when it is appropriate. God, in Your sovereignty, You gave me the mother and father that You did. May I honor You as I honor them. Amen.

Honour thy father and thy mother, as the LORD thy God hath commanded thee.
DEUTERONOMY 5:16

Avoiding Idleness

Lord, I know that You want me to take care of my household. Sometimes I am so tempted to put off my duties around the house, and I find myself spending too much time on my computer or my phone. Help me to be balanced. Help me to take care of my household and to be aware of the trap of idleness. I know that procrastination is not a good or godly habit. Amen.

She looketh well to the ways of her household, and eateth not the bread of idleness.
PROVERBS 31:27

Every Good Gift

Father, thank You for the blessings You have poured out on my family. Often I dwell on what we do not have. Please remind me to be ever grateful for so many gifts. The comforts we enjoy each day like running water and electricity are so easily taken for granted. Thank You for Your provision in our lives. Help me to have a thankful heart so that my family might be more thankful also. Amen.

And thou shalt rejoice in every good thing which the Lord thy God hath given unto thee, and unto thine house, thou, and the Levite, and the stranger that is among you.
Deuteronomy 26:11

My Church Family

My church is special to me in so many ways, Lord. I am so thankful that You have placed me among such a wonderful group of believers who encourage me and pray for me. Allow me to be a blessing to them as well, and help me to never forget how important they are in my life.

For our comely parts have no need: but God hath tempered the body together, having given more abundant honour to that part which lacked. That there should be no schism in the body; but that the members should have the same care one for another. And whether one member suffer, all the members suffer with it; or one member be honoured, all the members rejoice with it. Now ye are the body of Christ, and members in particular.

1 CORINTHIANS 12:24–27

My Pastor

Thank You for my pastor, dear God. He loves You; and he loves those to whom he ministers. Knowing that his desire is to present the truths of the Bible is a great comfort in a world that is full of false teachings. Bless my pastor as he continues to preach Your Word.

And he gave some, apostles; and some, prophets; and some, evangelists; and some, pastors and teachers; for the perfecting of the saints, for the work of the ministry, for the edifying of the body of Christ.
EPHESIANS 4:11–12

The Value of Fellowship

Heavenly Father, I pray that You will not allow me to isolate myself. I need fellowship with other believers. I benefit from spending time with my Christian friends. You tell us in Your Word that it is not good to be alone. We need one another as we walk through this life with all of its ups and downs. When I am tempted to distance myself from others, guide me back into Christian fellowship. Amen.

Two are better than one; because they have a good reward for their labour. For if they fall, the one will lift up his fellow.
ECCLESIASTES 4:9–10

Iron Sharpens Iron

Lord, I find it hard to talk to my friends about areas of their lives in which they are not honoring You. And I certainly do not always appreciate their correction in my life! Father, allow such sweet, godly fellowship between my Christian sisters and me that when truth should be spoken in love, we are able to speak into one another's lives. We need one another. Iron sharpens iron. Amen.

Iron sharpeneth iron; so a man sharpeneth the countenance of his friend.
PROVERBS 27:17

Shield of Faith

God, guard my heart and mind with the shield of faith. I will call on the name of Jesus when Satan tempts me. I will fight against his schemes to ruin me. My weapon is my knowledge of Your Word, promises memorized and cherished. My defense is my faith in Jesus Christ, my Savior. On this faith I will stand. Increase my faith and protect me from the evil one, I pray. Amen.

Above all, taking the shield of faith,
wherewith ye shall be able to quench
all the fiery darts of the wicked.
EPHESIANS 6:16

A Beautiful Work

Lord, I read of the woman who poured out a flask of expensive perfume on Your feet. The disciples did not understand, but You saw it as a beautiful work. Give me a heart like hers. Whatever I possess, whatever comes my way, help me to fling it all forth for Your glory. Let me use it wisely but extravagantly to honor my King. I love You, Lord. Make my life a beautiful work for You. Amen.

But when his disciples saw it, they had indignation, saying, To what purpose is this waste? For this ointment might have been sold for much, and given to the poor. When Jesus understood it, he said unto them, Why trouble ye the woman? for she hath wrought a good work upon me.
MATTHEW 26:8–10

Joyful Regardless of Circumstances

Lord, there are days when I can't help but rejoice in what You are doing. But many times the daily grind is just rather humdrum. There is nothing to rejoice about, much less give thanks for! Or is there? Help me, Father, to be joyful and thankful every day. Each day is a gift from You. Remind me of this truth today, and give me a joyful, thankful heart, I ask. Amen.

Rejoice evermore. Pray without ceasing.
In every thing give thanks: for this is the
will of God in Christ Jesus concerning you.
1 THESSALONIANS 5:16–18

A Meek and Quiet Spirit

God, in Your economy a meek and quiet spirit is worth more than gold. It is not corruptible. It is eternal. Give me such a spirit. Make me a better listener, I pray. Set a guard over my tongue at times when I should not speak. Teach me to walk humbly with You, Father, and to serve people in Your name. A gracious, godly spirit is what You desire to see in me. Amen.

Whose adorning let it not be that outward adorning of plaiting the hair, and of wearing of gold, or of putting on of apparel; but let it be the hidden man of the heart, in that which is not corruptible, even the ornament of a meek and quiet spirit, which is in the sight of God of great price.
1 PETER 3:3–4

A Witness in My Community

Lord, there are so many people in my community who either don't care about You or think they will please You by their own merit, but several of them don't truly know You. I ask You to open doors so I may witness to them. My prayer is that many will come to You.

But whoso hath this world's good, and seeth his brother have need, and shutteth up his bowels of compassion from him, how dwelleth the love of God in him?

1 JOHN 3:17

The Gift of Salvation

Dear Father, thank You for the gift of salvation, for sending Your only Son to be a sacrifice for all people, even those who didn't want Him. I am in awe of Your mercy extended to me. It is incredible to think that I am a daughter of God. Thank You, Jesus; You didn't walk away from the cross, but You laid down Your life for me. Thank You, Holy Spirit, for drawing me to this greatest of gifts. My life is forever changed. In Christ's name, amen.

---

*For the grace of God has appeared
that offers salvation to all people.*
Titus 2:11 niv

A Father

God, help me remember that You're my Father. A heavenly Father—one who has unlimited resources and power and one who has infinitely more love than any great earthly dad. When Satan tempts me to view You with suspicion, help me remember that his goal is my utter destruction. Lord, fill my heart with the truth that You love me perfectly and have only the best in mind for me. In fact, You want to embrace me, bless me, and give me heaven as my inheritance. What a wonderful Father You are! Amen.

As a father has compassion on his children, so the Lord has compassion on those who fear him.
PSALM 103:13 NIV

Filled with Contentment

Sometimes my attitude is so "poor me" that I even get sick, Father. I keep thinking that if only I could have this or that, life would be easier. I know I'm missing out on a truly abundant life by whining so much, and I ask You to forgive me. Fill me with contentment. Amen.

Not that I speak in respect of want:
for I have learned, in whatsoever state
I am, therewith to be content.
PHILIPPIANS 4:11

A Perfect Place

Creator God, I wish there weren't diseases in our world. Those tiny microbes that infiltrate the immune system are responsible for so much pain and grief. Although sickness was not present in the garden of Eden—that perfect place You intended for us—it is a part of this life now, a consequence of the curse under which our world suffers. But someday You'll create a new earth, and I know bacteria won't stand a chance there. I look forward to that, Father God, for then the world will once again be "very good." Amen.

*Now I saw a new heaven and a
new earth, for the first heaven and
the first earth had passed away.*
REVELATION 21:1 NKJV

Internal Clocks

Heavenly Father, it seems like every person has an internal rhythm seemingly permanently set to a certain time of the day. There are early birds and night owls and middle-of-the-day people. Not many of us are successful in changing our internal clock, Lord. Maybe You wanted to create humans with varying peak hours of energy. It would be a pretty boring world if we all fizzled out at the same time each day. Thank You for the variety You have provided in all of us. Amen.

To declare Your lovingkindness in the morning, and Your faithfulness every night.
PSALM 92:2 NKJV

Never Give Up

Lord, I don't want to be a quitter, but I've tried so hard to be like You, and I keep messing up. I know You said that with You all things are possible, and I need to be reminded of that daily. Don't let me give up. Help me to remember that You aren't finished with me yet. Amen.

Wherefore, my beloved, as ye have always obeyed, not as in my presence only, but now much more in my absence, work out your own salvation with fear and trembling. For it is God which worketh in you both to will and to do of his good pleasure.
PHILIPPIANS 2:12–13

Fitness

It's an exercise-crazy world we live in, Lord. Gym memberships are prized, morning jogs are eulogized, and workout clothing has become a fashion statement. There are some who make this area of self-care too important; they spend an inordinate amount of time on it. Yet others don't keep it high enough on their priority list. Help me, God, to keep the proper perspective of fitness, because, after all, I have a responsibility for the upkeep on this body. It's on loan from You. Amen.

Bodily fitness has a certain value, but spiritual fitness is essential both for this present life and for the life to come.
1 TIMOTHY 4:8 PHILLIPS

Slice of Life

Dear Lord, the transition of minutes to hours is so incremental that it is tedious to observe. It's much easier to focus on large chunks of time than myriad tiny ones. Yet hours are made up of minutes, just like the body is comprised of cells. Each is vital to the whole. Lord, help me remember that each minute of the day is a small section, a slice of my life. Help me make the best use of every minute. Amen.

*Make the best use of your time, despite
all the difficulties of these days.*
EPHESIANS 5:16 PHILLIPS

Strength to Stand

Lord, as large as my family is, there are bound to be some members whose life views are significantly different from mine. At times this gets annoying, particularly when they attempt to force their outlook on me. Give me the strength to stand for what I know to be true, and help me love my family despite our differences.

In the day when I cried thou answeredst me, and strengthenedst me with strength in my soul.

PSALM 138:3

Getting Started

Dear Lord, the first step toward any goal is the hardest, and I just don't feel motivated to take it. But there are things I need to do, and so far I haven't found a fairy to do them for me. Procrastination is a terrible hindrance. I know. I'm a closet procrastinator. I don't like to admit to it, but You see it anyway. Thank You for giving me more chances than I deserve. Remind me that I just need to start. Inspiration often springs from soil watered with obedience. Let me learn this lesson well. Amen.

The way of the sluggard is blocked with thorns.
PROVERBS 15:19 NIV

Difficult People

Dear Lord, I ask You to help me be patient and kind today. The Bible speaks about long-suffering. That's what I need as I deal with difficult people and irritating situations. Whether it's squabbling children or rude drivers or harried clerks, I know there will be those today who will irk me. In those moments when I want to scream, help me remember to forbear and forgive. It's just so easy to react, but help me instead to deliberately choose my response. I'm depending on Your power, Father. Amen.

Bear with each other and forgive one another if any of you has a grievance against someone.
COLOSSIANS 3:13 NIV

Wise Fear

"The fear of the LORD is the beginning of wisdom" (Psalm 111:10). Sometimes this passage from Your Word seems almost contradictory, Lord. But there is healthy fear, and then there's crippling fear. I know this passage means that my respect of You is so deep that I abhor sin. Please help me to have this wise fear. Amen.

The fear of the LORD is the beginning of wisdom: and the knowledge of the holy is understanding.
PROVERBS 9:10

Unlimited Resources

Father, the Bible says You own "the cattle on a thousand hills." You have unlimited resources. So I'm asking You to supply a special need I have today. Although I try to be a good steward of the money You give me, some unexpected event has caught me without the necessary funds. I know You can remedy this situation, if You deem that good for me. Because You're my Father, I'm asking for Your financial advice. I need Your wisdom in this area of my life. Amen.

"For every animal of the forest is mine, and the cattle on a thousand hills."
PSALM 50:10 NIV

Lost!

Lord, I've lost my cell phone again! Please help me find it! I know sometimes I'm careless; help me learn from this. But, Lord, You know how much information is in that phone and how much I need it to carry out my responsibilities today. You know where it is right now. Help me think of that place. Guide me to it. And just like the woman with the lost coin—I will rejoice! Amen.

"Rejoice with me, for I have found the piece which I lost!"
LUKE 15:9 NKJV

A Proper Outlook

So often, Lord, I see relationships crumbling, and much of the time a money issue is what starts the process. Some people are careless or dishonest in their spending; others just want too much. As a result there is a lot of bitterness and hatred. Please help me to have a proper outlook when money is involved.

He that loveth silver shall not be satisfied with silver; nor he that loveth abundance with increase: this is also vanity.
ECCLESIASTES 5:10

God Is a Shield

Protector God, today I'm remembering someone in the armed forces. Though I know war wasn't in Your original plan for this world, it has become a necessary tool for overcoming evil. The Bible recounts stories of You leading Your people, the Israelites, into battle to defend what was right. So there is honor in defending freedom and justice. I ask You to protect this one from danger; dispatch Your peace, and put a hedge before, behind, and around him. Watch over all those who are putting their lives in harm's way for my sake. In Christ's name, amen.

He shields all who take refuge in him
. . . . He trains my hands for battle;
my arms can bend a bow of bronze.
You make your saving help my shield.
PSALM 18:30, 34–35 NIV

A Shining Light

Dear God, I want to be a better witness for You. I have friends and family members who don't know You, and every day I interact with people who aren't believers. Lord, I don't want to be corny or pushy, but I do want to let my light shine before others. I ask You to open up the doors for me today. Let me sense Your prompting. And let the silent witness of my life also speak to others about Your great plan of salvation. In Jesus' name, amen.

"Let your light so shine before men,
that they may see your good works and
glorify your Father in heaven."
MATTHEW 5:16 NKJV

Extras

Dear God, I am so thankful that You have provided for me. Sometimes that blessing even goes above and beyond my needs. I now ask for wisdom in handling these gifts. My desire is to glorify You and to make sure that I'm not controlled by money. Please help me use it in a way that honors You. Amen.

But my God shall supply all your need according to his riches in glory by Christ Jesus.
PHILIPPIANS 4:19

Keep Me

Dear Father, in the scurry of life, I often forget to be thankful for important things. So many times You've shielded my family from physical harm, and I didn't know it until later. And I'm sure I don't even know about all those moments when You've guarded us from spiritual danger. Although we are the apple of Your eye, I realize we're not immune to trauma and disaster. You won't remove the effects of the curse until the right time comes. But for now, I'm grateful that You care about us and that the only way something can touch us is after it's passed Your gentle inspection. Amen.

Keep me as the apple of the eye, hide me under the shadow of thy wings.
PSALM 17:8

51

Role Reversal

Dear Lord, when I was growing up, my parents seemed ageless. But I realize now that my time with them is getting shorter every day. They're getting older, Lord; and, more and more, I find myself looking out for them. This role reversal is really difficult for me. I'm accustomed to them looking out for me, and part of me wishes I could stay in their care for a while longer. Please give me strength to deal with this new phase of our relationship, and help me honor them as long as they live and beyond. Amen.

"Even to your old age, I am He,
and even to gray hairs I will carry
you! I have made, and I will bear;
even I will carry, and will deliver you."
Isaiah 46:4 nkjv

Natural Consequences

Dear Lord, I know You've forgiven me for that horrible wrong. I thought when I repented that would take care of things, but I'm learning that the natural consequences still hurt. I know they won't disappear, but I pray that You will use them in a positive way—perhaps to keep others from making the same mistake. Amen.

Blessed is he whose transgression is forgiven, whose sin is covered.
PSALM 32:1

Spiritual Guardrails

Dear God, help me erect proper boundaries in my life. I don't want to fall prey to a sin simply because I wasn't being careful. Just like guardrails on a dangerous mountain highway, boundaries in my life keep me closer to center and farther away from the cliffs. I know Satan is plotting my destruction, but Your power is greater. Let me cooperate with Your grace by a careful lifestyle and a discerning spirit. In Christ's name, amen.

Stay alert! Watch out for your great enemy,
the devil. He prowls around like a roaring
lion, looking for someone to devour.
1 PETER 5:8 NLT

Cheerfulness

Jesus, I can't imagine You as a sour, solemn man. I believe You enjoyed life immensely, and I know You brought joy to those around You. Why else would "sinners and tax collectors" want to eat with You (as Your enemies pointed out)? Your mission on this planet was sacred and grave, but I believe Your demeanor in everyday life was buoyant and pleasant. Others loved being in Your presence. Help me pattern my daily attitude after Your example and take heed of Your command to "be of good cheer." Let me reflect You by the way I approach living. Amen.

"Be of good cheer, daughter."
MATTHEW 9:22 NKJV

Blessed Are
the Flexible

Flexibility is a struggle for me, God. I don't like interruptions in my routine. It's challenging for me to accept a rerouting of my day. Still, sometimes, You have to reorganize for me because I haven't recognized Your promptings. Or maybe there's someone You need me to meet or a disaster You want me to avoid. Help me accept the detours in my plan today, aware of Your sovereignty over all. Amen.

This is the day the LORD has made;
we will rejoice and be glad in it.
PSALM 118:24 NKJV

Lord, Carry My Friend

My friend is hurting, dear Jesus. She's had so many struggles in her life lately, and she feels like she's about to hit rock bottom. I've tried to be there for her, but right now she needs You in a special way. Please let her know that You want to carry her through this trial. Help her trust You. Amen.

A friend loveth at all times.
PROVERBS 17:17

Just Do It

Dear Lord, I want to have an obedient heart. Sometimes, when You speak to me, I feel hesitation or want to postpone what You're telling me to do. Yet that means either I don't trust You or I want my own way, neither of which is good. A child ought to obey her parents because she acknowledges their right to direct her and because she trusts the love behind the words. Help me, Lord, to embrace that kind of attitude when You speak to me. In Christ's name, amen.

But be doers of the word, and not hearers only, deceiving yourselves.
JAMES 1:22 NKJV

The Simple Life

Dear God, simplicity is a buzzword today. It seems everyone wants "simple" in some fashion. Perhaps it's because life has become too complicated for many of us; we yearn for a more laid-back lifestyle. Lord, I need to simplify my goals in my relationships and my work. Doing so will help me to have a more laser-like focus. And in my spiritual life, a little simplifying might be good too. Instead of trying to conquer large portions of scripture daily, help me to focus on a few verses, thus letting me steadily grow in understanding. Lord, help me keep simple goals and a simple faith as I simply live for You. Amen.

Aspire to lead a quiet life, to mind your own business, and to work with your own hands.
1 THESSALONIANS 4:11 NKJV

Reached Goals

Sometimes I get a little discouraged, Jesus. I feel like I've reached all the goals I've set for myself and that there's nothing for me to achieve that would bring any excitement. Please give me a new outlook. Give me wisdom as I set new goals, and help me give You the glory when I succeed. Amen.

For wisdom is better than rubies; and all the things that may be desired are not to be compared to it.
PROVERBS 8:11

Meekness

Heavenly Father, I want to develop the characteristic of meekness, a kind of quiet strength. Rather than a sign of a pushover, meekness is a trait of the strong. It takes guts to be silent when you want to speak. Meekness is not a goal for the weak of heart. It is, rather, for those who would be in the forefront of spiritual growth. Like Moses, the meekest man on earth (see Numbers 12:3), we can reap the rewards of quiet strength in our lives. Amen.

With all lowliness and meekness, with longsuffering, forbearing one another in love.
EPHESIANS 4:2

Legacy

Dear God, what kind of legacy am I leaving? I want to be remembered as more than a woman who dressed nicely, had a great family, and went to church. I want to be remembered for the way I invested myself in the lives of others. After all, love is the only lasting thing on this earth, something that will remain when I am physically gone but living with You in eternity. Lord, let my legacy be wrapped up in serving others in love. In Jesus' name, amen.

Prophecy and speaking in unknown languages and special knowledge will become useless. But love will last forever!
1 CORINTHIANS 13:8 NLT

Hospitality

Dear Lord, I need to improve my skills in hospitality. Because You have blessed me, I need to share with others. In fact, hospitality is one of those virtues the apostle Paul commanded of the church. Sharing my home with others is my Christian duty and also a great way to reach out to unbelievers whom I have befriended. Please let me not dread hosting others but rather find ways to make it doable and enjoyable for all. In Jesus' name, amen.

---

*Use hospitality one to another
without grudging.*
1 PETER 4:9

Consulting Christ

Lord, often in my daily planning I forget to consult You. Then I wonder why things don't work out the way I think they should. Forgive my arrogant attitude. I know that only as You guide me through the day will I find joy in accomplishments. Show me how to align my goals with Your will. Amen.

---

*Trust in the LORD with all thine heart;
and lean not unto thine own understanding.*
PROVERBS 3:5

Sensory Joys

Dear God, thank You for the five senses—sight, sound, touch, smell, and taste. You could have designed a virtual world, but instead You created one that can be experienced. Today I want to revel in the fact that I'm alive. I want to delight in the tactile joys I often take for granted. I'm grateful for each one. Amen.

For in him we live, and move,
and have our being.
ACTS 17:28

The Real Me

Heavenly Father, so many people in my world wear masks. We earth dwellers are afraid to be real with others; we fear losing the respect and esteem of our peers. And, oddly enough, we're often afraid to be real with even You— and You know everything about us anyway. I want to be genuine in my approach and interaction with others, including You. Give me the courage to reject the lure of artificial "perfectness" and instead live out my life and relationships in a real way. Amen.

I have chosen the way of truth.
PSALM 119:30 NKJV

Time Management

Dear God, sometimes I think I need more than twenty-four hours in my day! It seems I never have enough time. I think with longing about simpler seasons in my life when I could actually complete my to-do lists. There was such satisfaction in having a few stress-free moments. Now, my schedule is filled, and I'm so harried. Holy Spirit, please guide in this area of my life. How I use my time is part of stewardship, so I'm asking for Your wisdom. Show me how to manage the hours I have so I can honor You in everything I do. In Christ's name, amen.

Teach us to number our days, that we may gain a heart of wisdom.
PSALM 90:12 NIV

The Power of Words

Father, my mouth sometimes gets me into trouble. Please keep me aware of the things I say that aren't right. Let me back up and apologize if I've hurt anyone. Better yet, let me consider my words before I cast them out on the wind. Once spoken, they can never be recalled. Your written Word is living, brilliant, and powerful; Jesus is the embodiment of it—the living Word. My spoken earthly words are weighty as well; they can minister life or death to those who hear. I ask You to remind me of this throughout the day. Amen.

Death and life are in the power of the tongue: and they that love it shall eat the fruit thereof.
PROVERBS 18:21

First Glimpse of Gray

Lord, I found a gray hair today. I guess I could call it silver (not good) or white (even worse). Whatever the tint is, it's not the color I was born with! I realize the aging process is part of the death process and death in our world is the result of sin. So, I feel perfectly justified in not wanting to age. But I must acknowledge the fact that I cannot continually stay in the youthful season of life. Please give me whatever kind of grace I need to resist adopting a nasty attitude about growing older, and renew my strength every day. Amen.

The outward man does indeed suffer wear and tear, but every day the inward man receives fresh strength.
2 Corinthians 4:16 phillips

Food Budgeting

God, I'm really struggling today with self-worth because I just feel so fat. I know I need discipline—to eat less and exercise more. I do pretty well for a while, but then I get off track. And dieting feels like fake living. I mean, who seriously thinks fat-free cheese is delicious? I see skinny people every day who can wear stylish clothing and aren't afraid to stand in the front row when group pictures are taken. I want that kind of freedom, Lord, so help me "budget" my food so I can rid myself of feeling overblown. Amen.

But the fruit of the Spirit is. . .self-control.
GALATIANS 5:22–23 NIV

Gossip

Lord, I got caught in gossip today. I didn't mean to though. A group of us were just talking about this and that, and You know how women are. We're so into relationships and what others are doing. Before long, the conversation had dug itself a little too deep into someone else's life. I tried to stop listening but didn't try hard enough. By the time we broke up our little gabfest, I felt terribly guilty. Please forgive me, Father. Give me the courage to make the right decision next time; help me refuse to listen to negative stories about those who are not there to defend themselves. In Jesus' name, amen.

*Let all. . .evil speaking be put away
from you, with all malice.*
EPHESIANS 4:31 NKJV

Fixing My Thoughts

God, today I'm having a pity party. My thoughts are so focused on earthly things that I am having trouble looking up. I could mope around here all day, but I guess it's time for the music to stop and the party to end. Lord, You can't work through me when I'm feeling sorry for myself. Forgive me for my pettiness, and let me respond to life with maturity. Help me focus on good, praiseworthy things. In Christ's name, amen.

---

*Fix your thoughts on what is true,
and honorable, and right, and pure,
and lovely, and admirable.*
PHILIPPIANS 4:8 NLT

Music

Dear Lord, music is the universal language of the human family. Today, music is available on a multitude of electronic devices. And there are so many genres—an array of listening options. Some appeal to me; others don't. But I want to base my choices on Your principles. What I listen to will affect my mood, my attitude, and my spiritual state of being. Holy Spirit, give me discernment. Let the music I listen to not go counter to what You're trying to do in me. Amen.

Whatsoever ye do, do all to the glory of God.
1 CORINTHIANS 10:31

Coveting

God, it's so easy to break the tenth commandment: Do not covet (see Exodus 20:17). Coveting is a way of life for many in our world. But You say we shouldn't compare ourselves with the Joneses, nor envy them and what they have. Whatever You've given me is to be enjoyed and received, not held up for inspection. Teach me a deeper gratefulness for Your blessings. In Jesus' name, amen.

Let your conduct be without covetousness.
HEBREWS 13:5 NKJV

The Same Old Me

Lord, today I come to You a bit discouraged. The traits I see in myself are ones I don't like. It seems I could do much more for You without some of the inherent flaws of my personality. So help me overcome my defects, or use me in spite of them. Help me to love myself, as imperfect as I am, and to strive to be the best me I can be. I know You can find a way around my impediments and use me for Your glory, just like You used Moses in spite of his speech problem. Amen.

You have searched me, Lord,
and you know me.
Psalm 139:1 NIV

Blank Stares

Today I'm struggling, Jesus. I have a specific goal that needs to be met, but it requires clarity of mind. The project is spread out before me, but I'm staring at it blankly. I know You want me to work on it, and I need Your guidance. Give me the ability to think and complete the task. Amen.

In all thy ways acknowledge him,
and he shall direct thy paths.
PROVERBS 3:6

Golden Words Needed

Heavenly Father, today I need affirming words. You know that words are important to me as a woman. You also know that I struggle with self-worth. The other people in my world don't always meet my need to be affirmed verbally, and I can't expect them to fulfill every void in my life. So, Lord, let me look to and in Your Word to find the love and encouragement I need. In Jesus' name, amen.

A word fitly spoken is like apples of gold in settings of silver.
PROVERBS 25:11 NKJV

Poise

Heavenly Father, I need poise—that kind of gracious manner and behavior that characterized women of past generations. It seems to be disdained in my culture. Women now are expected and encouraged to be free spirits—unrestricted by convention and decorum. But I cringe when I observe women using crude language, slouching in their seats, and adopting careless ways of walking and eating. I don't want to seem prissy and uppity, but I do want to guard against being too informal. Help me develop the traits that portray womanhood as the gentle, beautiful, fascinating gender You designed. Amen.

Like a gold ring in a pig's snout is a beautiful woman who shows no discretion.
PROVERBS 11:22 NIV

Lessons in Trust

Heavenly Father, teach me to trust. I know it's an area of weakness for me. In spite of the fact that I know Your character and Your track record, I find it so difficult to relinquish to You the important areas of life. Oh, I say that I will, and I do put forth effort to rely on You, but we both know that, in my heart, I find it hard to let You handle everything. So take my hand, Lord, and teach me to trust. You're the Master; I am forever Your student. In Christ's name, amen.

I have put my trust in the Lord GOD,
that I may declare all Your works.
PSALM 73:28 NKJV

Special Instructions

Thank You for Your Word, Father. Without it I would be a helpless cause in regard to developing godly character. I'm so glad You preserved these special words that give me specific instruction on how to live. Help me to hide these scriptures in my heart so that I'm able to rely on them throughout my life. Amen.

---

*Thy word is a lamp unto my feet,
and a light unto my path.*
PSALM 119:105

Divine Guidance

Dear Lord, it's so hard sometimes to know what Your will is. You don't write specific instructions in the sky nor emblazon them on a marquee. So how can I know exactly what You want me to do? How can I keep from making a big mistake? How can I proceed with this decision? I ask today that You would give me wisdom; please send me guidance as I seek Your will. Through a person, a thought, a scripture, let me sense Your leading for this situation. I want my life to honor Your plan for me. In Christ's name, amen.

If any of you lacks wisdom, you should ask God, who gives generously to all without finding fault, and it will be given to you.
JAMES 1:5 NIV

81

Things Not Seen

Jesus, it is easy to believe in what I can see. I wish I could reach out and touch You. As I meditate on Your Word, give me faith in what I cannot see. Give me faith that all of Your promises are true and that one day You will come again in the clouds to take me home. Amen.

Now faith is the substance of things hoped for, the evidence of things not seen.
HEBREWS 11:1

God Is Faithful

God, I focus a lot on my faith in You. And then You show me that it is not all about me. You are faithful to me. You show me how to be faithful. You never leave. You never give up on me. You never turn away. You always show up. You always believe in me. You are faithful by Your very nature. You cannot be unfaithful. Thank You for Your faithfulness in my life. Amen.

But the Lord is faithful, who shall stablish you, and keep you from evil.
2 Thessalonians 3:3

Being Godly on Purpose

Lord, I was recently reminded that godly character doesn't just happen. I have to purpose in my heart to live a life pleasing to You. Only then will I be able to stand strong when peer pressure threatens to undo me. I want to commit daily to obeying You. Amen.

And be not conformed to this world:
but be ye transformed by the renewing of your
mind, that ye may prove what is that good,
and acceptable, and perfect, will of God.
ROMANS 12:2

Resting on the Sabbath

Father, You created us as beings who work and need rest. Sometimes I forget that. I get so caught up in all that must be accomplished. Slow my pace, Lord. Help me to honor You by resting one day per week. Help me to keep the Sabbath holy. Thank You for designing the week and for telling Your people to rest. It is up to me to follow Your command. Amen.

Remember the sabbath day, to keep it holy.
Six days shalt thou labour, and do all thy work:
but the seventh day is the sabbath of the Lord
thy God: in it thou shalt not do any work.
EXODUS 20:8–10

Restored

God, I'm grappling with failure. In something in which I wanted so badly to succeed, I've had a less than stellar performance. In fact, humiliating is more like it. I've failed to accomplish my own goals. And I've disappointed others I care about. So where do I go from here? I'm not a quitter, yet I admit I'm lacking motivation to try again. Please give me the courage I need, and help me remember all those Bible characters who refused to be defined by failure but instead sought grace, attempted the challenge again, and triumphed. Let my story be like theirs, I pray. In Jesus' name, amen.

Restore to me the joy of Your salvation,
and uphold me by Your generous Spirit.
PSALM 51:12 NKJV

Saved by Grace through Faith

God, it is so comforting to know that my position before You is secure. Thank You for seeing me through a new lens. When You look at me, because I have been saved through faith, You see Your Son in me. You no longer see sin but righteousness. I couldn't have earned it, no matter how hard I worked. Thank You for the gift of salvation through my faith in Jesus. Amen.

For by grace are ye saved through faith;
and that not of yourselves: it is the gift of God:
not of works, lest any man should boast.
EPHESIANS 2:8–9

The Center of God's Will

Lord, I know that in the center of Your will are peace, joy, and many other rich blessings. I'd like to experience all these things, but the trouble I seem to have is figuring out what Your will is for me. Please help me be attentive when You speak, and give me a heart willing to be used by You. Amen.

Commit thy works unto the LORD,
and thy thoughts shall be established.
PROVERBS 16:3

The Heart of Giving

Jesus, You see the heart of the giver. I can imagine the shock of the disciples when You declared the widow's small gift greater than that of the rich. They gave of their excess. She gave all she had. She wanted to be part of the kingdom work. She trusted You to meet her needs. May I have a true giver's heart. May I give sacrificially as the widow did that day. Amen.

Verily I say unto you, That this poor widow hath cast more in, than all they which have cast into the treasury: for all they did cast in of their abundance; but she of her want did cast in all that she had, even all her living.

MARK 12:43–44

Trust in His Strength

Lord, at times I get cocky. I step out on my own and think I've got everything under control. But then something happens that shakes my world. I find myself calling on You and hoping You will come. You always show up. You always remember me. I am Your child. Help me to trust You before I am desperate. Help me to remember the source of my strength. Amen.

For I will not trust in my bow,
neither shall my sword save me.
PSALM 44:6

Deep Surrender

Lord, I need to surrender to You. You've shown me an area of my life that I've been trying to rule. I know You need the keys to every room in my heart, and so here I am, bringing this one to You. Surrender means I give You permission to change, clean out, and add things. Waving the white flag isn't really easy, but it's the way to true joy. Thank You for showing me that. Amen.

But now, O LORD, You are our Father;
we are the clay, and You our potter;
and all we are the work of Your hand.
ISAIAH 64:8 NKJV

Filled with Love

Lord, let my home be a comforting haven for my family and friends. May it be a place where they can momentarily escape the pressures of this world. Help me to do my best to make it a place where people will know they are loved by me and, more importantly, by You. Amen.

A new commandment I give unto you,
That ye love one another; as I have loved
you, that ye also love one another.
JOHN 13:34

To-Do Lists

God, I like to know what's coming up next in my life. I like to chart the items requiring some kind of action from me. To-do lists are my way of planning out the day and week. The lists keep me on track, but anything can be detrimental if it becomes too important. Help me not to plot and plan my life so completely that there is no room for divine interruptions, for Providence to intervene. Give me patience with those who cause my day to go awry; let me see beyond the irritation to what You have in mind. In Jesus' name, amen.

---

*We can make our plans, but the
LORD determines our steps.*
PROVERBS 16:9 NLT

Endurance Required

I'm finding, Lord, that the Christian life is one that requires endurance. It isn't enough to start well. So let me patiently and steadily move down the road to Christlikeness. I know difficulties will come; I've faced some already. It reminds me of the words of the second verse of "Amazing Grace": "Through many dangers, toils and snares, I have already come. 'Tis grace that brought me safe thus far, and grace will lead me home." In Your name, amen.

Let us run with endurance the race that is set before us.
HEBREWS 12:1 NKJV

Family Time

Thank You for my home, dear Jesus. I just love to be here. I can't explain the joy that comes from being surrounded by those I love. Whether our home is filled with laughter during game night or shrouded in silent contemplation during family devotions, I can feel Your presence, and I am uplifted. Amen.

Be kindly affectioned one to another with brotherly love; in honour preferring one another.
ROMANS 12:10

Criticism and Judging

Dear Lord, criticism can be so hurtful. It's easy to give, but so difficult to receive. Sometimes people paraphrase Matthew 7:1 as "Don't judge." But it actually means "Don't judge unless you want to be judged." I don't think we realize that when we criticize others, we open ourselves up to the same kind of scrutiny. I'm not very good at living up to this standard. Help me to be less critical of others. Check me, Holy Spirit, when I start to say something judgmental. Amen.

Set a guard over my mouth, LORD;
keep watch over the door of my lips.
PSALM 141:3 NIV

Granting Forgiveness

Heavenly Father, I need to forgive someone who wronged me. I know it's the right thing, but it's so difficult. I can't do it in my own strength. Give me the power to extend grace to this person. Put Your love in my heart so I can have a gracious attitude and heart of mercy. The Bible tells me to forgive because I have been forgiven. This is my chance to put it into practice. I'm leaning on Your power. In Jesus' name, amen.

"And whenever you stand praying, if you have anything against anyone, forgive him, that your Father in heaven may also forgive you your trespasses."
MARK 11:25 NKJV

Christ's Loneliness

Lord, how alone You must have been in the garden when the disciples fell asleep. And when God turned His back as You hung on the cross—was there anything to compare to what You felt? Yet You did it willingly. You understand when I'm lonely, and I thank You for being there during those times. Amen.

Fear thou not; for I am with thee: be not dismayed; for I am thy God: I will strengthen thee; yea, I will help thee; yea, I will uphold thee with the right hand of my righteousness.
ISAIAH 41:10

Delicate, Powerful Faith

God, faith is such a delicate concept, yet so mighty in its power. Faith isn't something I can wrap my arms around, but it is something I can rest my soul in. Hebrews 11:1 says it's "the evidence of things not seen." That means it's like a virtual item—something that already exists, though you can't hold it in your hand. Faith is sometimes trivialized in our world, but it is of utmost importance to You. Please increase my faith, O Lord. In Christ's name, amen.

Now faith is the substance of things hoped for, the evidence of things not seen.

HEBREWS 11:1

Power Boost

Dear God, please help me hold together the pieces of my life. My to-do list seems endless. There is always someone needing me. There are constant demands on my energy and sanity. I feel like I go through life in a state of exhaustion. I know that keeps me from being at my peak. And I know You want me to care for my health. But I'm stuck in a cycle of busyness that has no end in sight. Show me what I can change, Lord. Show me how to get the emotional and physical wellness I need. Amen.

He gives power to the weak, and to those who have no might He increases strength. . . . Those who wait on the LORD shall renew their strength; they shall mount up with wings like eagles, they shall run and not be weary, they shall walk and not faint.
ISAIAH 40:29, 31 NKJV

Tears

I've heard, God, that tears speak their own language. If that's true, then You made women verbal in two ways—words and tears. Being the gentler, more emotional reflection of Your image, we tend to cry easily. Like most women, I cry for a variety of reasons, and sometimes for no reason at all, like today. But since You read what's in my heart, I know You understand. Thank You for valuing my tears. Amen.

Put my tears into Your bottle;
are they not in Your book?
PSALM 56:8 NKJV

A Friendlier World

Dear God, I was just noticing all the people around me who really could use a friend. For whatever reason, they're alone and hurting. I need to reach out to them. I ask You to give me opportunities and ideas to let them know I care. Let me make the world a little friendlier for them. Amen.

Finally, be ye all of one mind, having compassion one of another, love as brethren, be pitiful, be courteous.
1 PETER 3:8

Anger

God, I need a solution for my anger. Sometimes I let it take over then end up regretting what it leads me to say or do. As I pray and study and grow closer to You, show me ways to control it. Guide me to the right verses to memorize and incorporate into my life. Lead me to someone who can keep me accountable. And, most of all, help me strive for self-control. Amen.

*If it is possible, as much as depends
on you, live peaceably with all men.
Beloved, do not avenge yourselves,
but rather give place to wrath;
for it is written, "Vengeance is Mine,
I will repay," says the Lord.*
ROMANS 12:18–19 NKJV

Never Really Alone

Heavenly Father, I'm lonely today. There is no one with whom I can share what is going on in my life right now. Oh, I have friends, but no one who would really understand this. But You created me, and You know me like no one else. I ask You today to let me feel Your presence with me. It's a terrible thing to be alone, but You promised You'd never leave. So, I know You are with me. I'm grateful for Your constant love and care. In Jesus' name, amen.

God has said: "I will never leave you nor forsake you."
HEBREWS 13:5 PHILLIPS

Buoyancy of Faith

God, I've seen swollen rivers; I've watched raging water destroy entire communities. And right now, I feel like the tide of my life is reaching flood level. I'm struggling to keep my head above water, but the waves keep crashing over me. This struggle with depression is almost more than I can bear. Sometimes I just want to surrender to the current and slip under the water. But others are depending on me, and You would be hurt if I chose to end this journey that way. Please hold me up in this flood; Your hands are the only ones that can. Amen.

"When you pass through the waters, I will be with you; and through the rivers, they shall not overflow you."
ISAIAH 43:2 NKJV

Provision for Missions

In Your Word, You've commanded us to take the gospel to all nations. You've also said that when we're obedient, You'll meet our needs. Please meet the needs of our missionaries, Lord. Provide what they need physically and spiritually, and let many souls be saved as a result.

Therefore take no thought, saying, What shall we eat? or, What shall we drink? or, Wherewithal shall we be clothed? . . . For your heavenly Father knoweth that ye have need of all these things.
MATTHEW 6:31–32

A Godly Example

God, help me to be an example of a faithful disciple of Christ to my family and friends. Those who are close in our lives have the ability to lead us toward or away from righteousness and godliness. I pray that all I do and say will honor You and that I will never be a stumbling block to others. May all within my sphere of influence find me faithful to You. Amen.

The righteous is more excellent than his neighbour: but the way of the wicked seduceth them.

PROVERBS 12:26

Joy in the Name
of the Lord

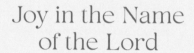

Father, this morning I meet You here for just
a few moments before the busyness of the day
takes over. I trust You. It is not always easy to
trust, but You have proven Yourself trustworthy
in my life. I find joy in the knowledge that
You are my defender. You go before me this
day into battle. I choose joy today because I
love the name of the Lord Almighty. Amen.

---

*But let all those that put their trust in
thee rejoice: let them ever shout for joy,
because thou defendest them: let them also
that love thy name be joyful in thee.*

Psalm 5:11

Showing Mercy

Jesus, like the Good Samaritan in Your parable, may I too show mercy. Some may never enter the doors of a church, but what a difference an act of grace could make! Put before me opportunities to show unmerited favor. That is, after all, what You have shown to me. You died for my sins. I never could have earned salvation. It is a free gift, an act of grace. Make me merciful. Amen.

Which now of these three, thinkest thou, was neighbour unto him that fell among the thieves? And he said, He that shewed mercy on him. Then said Jesus unto him, Go, and do thou likewise.
LUKE 10:36–37

A God-Centered Home

Father, so many homes are shaken these days. So many families are shattering to pieces around me. Protect my home, I pray. Protect my loved ones. Be the foundation of my home, strong and solid, consistent and wise. May every decision made here reflect Your principles. May those who visit this home and encounter this family be keenly aware of our uniqueness, because we serve the one true and almighty God. Amen.

Except the LORD build the house, they labour in vain that build it: except the LORD keep the city, the watchman waketh but in vain.
PSALM 127:1

Invitation to Rest

Jesus, You told Your disciples to rest. You directed them to leave the crowd and to relax and eat. You saw that they had been busy with ministry and they needed to recuperate. If You directed them to rest, even these twelve who worked at Your side daily, You must want me to rest as well. Remind me to take breaks from ministry. I needed to hear that You give me permission to rest! Amen.

And he said unto them, Come ye yourselves apart into a desert place, and rest a while: for there were many coming and going, and they had no leisure so much as to eat.
MARK 6:31

God's Book of Wisdom

There are so many how-to books available today, Lord, and they all promise to increase my knowledge in some area. But not one of them gives any hope for added wisdom. Only Your Word offers that. Thank You for providing the means to know You more fully and to live life more abundantly. Amen.

For the word of the LORD is right;
and all his works are done in truth.
PSALM 33:4

Trust in His Guidance

Father, this morning I come before You and I praise You. You are good and loving. You have only my very best interests at heart. Take my hand and lead me. Show me the way to go. Like a child being carried in a loving parent's arms, let me relax and trust You. I know that You will never lead me astray. Thank You, God, for this assurance. Amen.

Cause me to hear thy lovingkindness in the morning; for in thee do I trust: cause me to know the way wherein I should walk; for I lift up my soul unto thee.
PSALM 143:8

Praying for Bold Faith

I desire a bold faith, Jesus. Like the woman who followed You, crying out, asking that You cast a demon from her daughter. She was a Gentile, not a Jew; yet she called You the Son of David. She acknowledged You as the Messiah. And You stopped. Her faith impressed You. You healed the child. May I be so bold. May I recognize that You are the only solution to every problem. Amen.

Then Jesus answered and said unto her,
O woman, great is thy faith: be it unto
thee even as thou wilt. And her daughter
was made whole from that very hour.
MATTHEW 15:28

Enjoyable Work

I'm blessed to have a job I enjoy, Lord. So many people aren't able to say the same, and many of them probably have good reason to dislike their work. Thank You for opening this door of opportunity for me. You've met my needs in a wonderful way. Amen.

Not with eyeservice, as menpleasers;
but as the servants of Christ, doing the will
of God from the heart; with good will doing
service, as to the Lord, and not to men.
EPHESIANS 6:6–7

Come to Jesus

I come to You, Lord Jesus. That is the first step. I come before You now in this quiet moment. As I begin this new day, calm my spirit. There is work that must be done today. But even as I work, I can find rest in You. Ease the tension and stress in me, Lord, as only You can do. Thank You for a sense of peace. Amen.

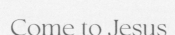

Come unto me, all ye that labour and are heavy laden, and I will give you rest.
MATTHEW 11:28

Following Christ's Example

Lord, You are always there, and You are consistently patient with me. What if it were not so? What if You reached Your limit and showed the wrath that I deserve in my sinful imperfection? Because of Your great patience with me, let me not grow tired of being patient myself. Let me model what You have shown me by Your example. Thank You for Your great patience with me, God. Amen.

And let us not be weary in well doing: for in due season we shall reap, if we faint not.
GALATIANS 6:9

Prioritizing

Father, I really have a lot to do, and I'm not very good at multitasking. I need Your help each day as I organize the chores that need to be done. Show me how to prioritize my workload so that I can get things done in the most efficient manner, and let my work be pleasing in Your sight. Amen.

But seek ye first the kingdom of God, and his righteousness; and all these things shall be added unto you.
MATTHEW 6:33

In Christ's Strength

Father, I am so thankful for the strength that is mine as a Christian. I cannot do anything on my own, but through Christ, I can do all things. It is comforting to know that the word *all* includes the trials and concerns that I bring to You this morning. I lay them at Your feet, Lord. I take You at Your Word. I can do all things through Jesus, who lives in me. Amen.

I can do all things through Christ which strengtheneth me.
PHILIPPIANS 4:13

Fear No Evil

How wonderful, God, that death has no power over the Christian! You are a strong and mighty God, the one true God. You are with me, protecting me all the way. And when the end of this life comes, whenever that may be, You will walk with me through the valley of the shadow of death. Death has lost its sting because Christ has conquered it! In Your name I pray. Amen.

Yea, though I walk through the valley of the shadow of death, I will fear no evil: for thou art with me; thy rod and thy staff they comfort me.
PSALM 23:4

God's Wisdom

I'm so forgetful! God, I know how many times You've admonished me to seek Your wisdom, yet over and over I try to do things on my own. You'd think I would learn after so many mistakes, but I guess I'm too proud. I don't want to continue like this. I want Your wisdom so that I can live life as You intended. Amen.

O the depth of the riches both of the wisdom and knowledge of God!
ROMANS 11:33

My Source of Strength

Father, at times I worry too much about what others think of me. Even when I just have a minor disagreement with a friend or coworker, I am afraid that the person will not like me anymore. I worry that I have not lived up to what was expected of me. Remind me, Father, that I must seek my ultimate strength and encouragement from You and You alone. Amen.

And David was greatly distressed; for the people spake of stoning him, because the soul of all the people was grieved, every man for his sons and for his daughters: but David encouraged himself in the LORD his God.

1 SAMUEL 30:6

Starting Where I Am

Jesus, You give tall orders! How can I teach all nations and baptize people? Oh. . .You mean I might not even have to leave my community? There are people all around me who don't know You, Lord. Help me to start with those in my sphere of influence. The grocery store clerk who seems tired and distraught. . .The teacher at my child's school who is so lost. . . Give me the courage to reach out. Amen.

Go ye therefore, and teach all nations,
baptizing them in the name of the Father,
and of the Son, and of the Holy Ghost.
MATTHEW 28:19

A Load of Stress

Deadlines, sports schedules, unexpected overnight company—I'm about to pull out my hair! I know we all have our share of stress, but didn't I get an extra load this week, Father? I'm not sure what the purpose of it is, but I know there's a reason. Lord, give me patience through the ordeal, and let me please You. Amen.

Take my yoke upon you, and learn of me; for I am meek and lowly in heart: and ye shall find rest unto your souls. For my yoke is easy, and my burden is light.
MATTHEW 11:29–30

Protection from Temptation

There is temptation all around me, Father. It is easy for me to say no to some of them. But there are subtle ways that Satan tempts me also. The movie that isn't appropriate. . .but all my friends are going to see. The newest style that is cute and fun. . .but a bit provocative for a Christian woman. Lord, keep my heart focused on You. Protect my heart from the influences of this world. Amen.

Can a man take fire in his bosom,
and his clothes not be burned?
PROVERBS 6:27

Serious Warning

Everywhere I look, Father, my society says it's okay. Sex before marriage and outside marriage. You warn us that this type of sin is of a serious nature. What we do with our bodies stays in our hearts and minds for a very long time. Protect me from the influences in my life that say these things are permissible when Your Word clearly states they are not good for me. Amen.

Flee fornication. Every sin that a man doeth is without the body; but he that committeth fornication sinneth against his own body.
1 CORINTHIANS 6:18

The Mission Field

Father, I believe the mission field You have for me is right here at home, but I know You want me to be involved in world missions as well. Help me faithfully pray for our missionaries. Give me wisdom as to how You would have me financially support them, and show me any other way I can help them. Amen.

It is more blessed to give than to receive.
ACTS 20:35

God Knows Me

God, the Bible says that You knew me even before I was formed in my mother's womb. I find confidence in this. You have been with me all along this journey! As I face this day, help me remember that I am never alone. You go before me to prepare the future. You walk with me through the present. And You were there with me since before I was born. Wow! Amen.

For thou hast possessed my reins: thou hast covered me in my mother's womb. I will praise thee; for I am fearfully and wonderfully made: marvellous are thy works; and that my soul knoweth right well.

PSALM 139:13–14

Martha's Trap

Lord, I want to be a servant, but I want it to be done Your way. Please don't let me get caught in Martha's trap of meeting only the physical needs. Although those elements are important, they don't reach the whole person. Let me be a blessing in the spiritual and emotional areas too. Amen.

Give, and it shall be given unto you; good measure, pressed down, and shaken together, and running over, shall men give into your bosom. For with the same measure that ye mete withal it shall be measured to you again.

LUKE 6:38

God Hears My Prayers

Lord, the gods of other religions are not approachable. Their subjects bow before them in anguish, hoping to find favor in their sight. These gods are not real. You are the one true and living God, a loving heavenly Father. I love that Your Word says I can come before You with confidence. You hear my prayers. You know my heart. Thank You, Father. Speak to my heart as I meditate on Your Word now. Amen.

And this is the confidence that we have in him, that, if we ask any thing according to his will, he heareth us.

1 JOHN 5:14

When to Remain Silent

Heavenly Father, Your Word says that the tongue has great power. My words can help or harm. There are times when silence is best. Help me know the difference between times I should speak and times I should keep still. I pray for wisdom as I go through this day. I want my speech to honor You. Put a guard over my lips, I pray. Amen.

In the multitude of words there wanteth not sin: but he that refraineth his lips is wise.
PROVERBS 10:19

Still Working on Me

Dear God, I'm a far cry from perfect, but I'm confident in the knowledge that You love me just as I am. You are the one who has begun a work in me, and You will be faithful to complete what has been started. What a thrill to know that You'll make me what You want me to be. Amen.

Let not mercy and truth forsake thee:
bind them about thy neck; write them
upon the table of thine heart.
PROVERBS 3:3

Applying Instruction

God, give me ears to hear. Sharpen my senses and make me wise. I am often proud. I think I know it all. But I don't. I need instruction from You. I know this comes in many forms... through reading and meditating on Your Word, through Your people, and through circumstances. Help me to be a good listener and to apply the instruction You send my way. I want to be wise, Father. Amen.

Hear counsel, and receive instruction,
that thou mayest be wise in thy latter end.
PROVERBS 19:20

Right Paths

The right path is often the one less traveled. I am learning this, Father, oh so slowly. You will always lead me in the right path. You will never lead me astray. I have been at the crossroads many times, and I will face such choices again and again. Keep my heart focused on You so that I might be led down pleasant paths, paths that will glorify my King. Amen.

I have taught thee in the way of wisdom;
I have led thee in right paths.
PROVERBS 4:11

Balancing Work and Rest

I had to chuckle as I read the verse that says, "Give not sleep to thine eyes" (Proverbs 6:4). I guess I don't have much trouble obeying that! I have more difficulty with "Come. . .apart. . . and rest a while" (Mark 6:31). I think I'm getting the picture, though. Please help me learn to balance work and rest. Amen.

My presence shall go with thee,
and I will give thee rest.
EXODUS 33:14

Generosity

Father, the psalmist declares that he has never seen the righteous forsaken or his children going hungry. This inspires me. I know that You bless those who give. I want to leave a legacy of generosity for my children or for others who are influenced by my life. What they see me practicing regarding giving will impact their choices. May we be a generous family, always looking for opportunities to show mercy. Amen.

I have been young, and now am old;
yet have I not seen the righteous forsaken,
nor his seed begging bread. He is ever
merciful, and lendeth; and his seed is blessed.
PSALM 37:25–26

A Woman Who Fears the Lord

God, I want to be a Proverbs 31 woman. My focus should not be on external beauty or the clothing and jewelry that I wear. Rather, may others notice my heart that is forever seeking You. I want nothing more than to be known as a woman of God. Protect me from vanity. Outward beauty is not lasting, but a beautiful spirit is. I meditate on Your Word now, Lord. I want to honor You. Amen.

Favour is deceitful, and beauty is vain: but a woman that feareth the LORD, she shall be praised.

PROVERBS 31:30

Christlikeness

There's such a fine line between self-esteem and arrogance. Sometimes I have trouble distinguishing between the two. Father, You created me in Your image. For that I am thankful, but I need to remember that I'm not perfect. Help me not to be proud but to daily strive to be more like You. Amen.

When pride cometh, then cometh shame:
but with the lowly is wisdom.
PROVERBS 11:2

Tithing

Father, You tell me to test You with my tithe. If I give it generously, You will bless my household. I will find it overflowing with blessing. There will not be enough room to contain all of it. I imagine the windows of heaven opening and blessings just pouring, pouring, pouring down on me! You are not a God who sprinkles blessings or gives them in little pinches or samples. You are an extravagant giver. Amen.

Bring ye all the tithes into the storehouse. . .
and prove me now herewith, saith the LORD
of hosts, if I will not open you the windows
of heaven, and pour you out a blessing.
MALACHI 3:10

A Testimony

My life is a song of praise to You, my faithful Father, the giver of life! When people hear my testimony of Your goodness, may they come to know You. I want others to notice the difference in me and wonder why I have such joy, such peace. May I point them to You, Lord, and may they trust in You for salvation. You are the way, the truth, and the life. Amen.

And he hath put a new song in my mouth, even praise unto our God: many shall see it, and fear, and shall trust in the LORD.

PSALM 40:3

Blessing Those
Who Hurt You

God, when someone hurts me, I don't feel like blessing that person. Remind me what Your Word teaches about love. Love keeps no record of wrongs. Love forgives. It restores. Love tries again. Love lets it go. Love blesses even when it's not my turn to bless! Give me a spirit of love that trumps evil. And allow me to bless those who hurt me. I can only do so in Your power. Amen.

Not rendering evil for evil, or railing for railing: but contrariwise blessing; knowing that ye are thereunto called, that ye should inherit a blessing.

1 PETER 3:9

In Harm's Way

Dear God, so many missionaries are in harm's way. They face terrorist threats, unsanitary living conditions, and even dangerous animals or illnesses that I can't begin to fathom. Please protect them, Father. They've willingly taken these risks so that others might know Your love. Keep them under Your wing of safety. Amen.

Unto the upright there ariseth light in the darkness: he is gracious, and full of compassion, and righteous.

PSALM 112:4

A Thankful Heart

Lord, everything good in my life comes from You. Often I forget to thank You. I am thankful for Your provision and Your protection. I am thankful for my family and friends. I am most of all thankful for the joy of my salvation, which comes through Christ. Give me a grateful heart, I pray. Let me always remember that every good and perfect gift comes from Your hand. Amen.

And let the peace of God rule in your hearts, to the which also ye are called in one body; and be ye thankful.
COLOSSIANS 3:15

All of Me

When You were asked what the greatest commandment was, You did not evade the question. You answered clearly, Jesus. I am to love the Lord my God with all of my heart, soul, mind, and strength. I am to love my God with all of me. There should be nothing left over when I am finished loving God. No crumbs to feed to the idols that crave my attention. It is all for You. Amen.

And thou shalt love the Lord thy God with all thy heart, and with all thy soul, and with all thy mind, and with all thy strength: this is the first commandment.
MARK 12:30

Special to the Father

How can I doubt my worth in Your eyes, Father? You know the number of hairs on my head. You created me, and You said that Your creation is very good. When I'm tempted to get down on myself, remind me that I am special to You and that there's no one just like me. Amen.

In the multitude of my thoughts within me thy comforts delight my soul.

PSALM 94:19

Love Covers Sins

Lord, all of my sin was nailed to the cross when Your Son died for me. Without grace, I am but filthy rags before a holy God. But through Christ, I am adopted as Your daughter, forgiven. There is pride in this daughter, God. Pride that resists forgiveness. Pride that says, "I am right." Remind me of the multitude of my own sins that Your love covered through Jesus. Help me love others well. Amen.

Hatred stirreth up strifes:
but love covereth all sins.
PROVERBS 10:12

Finding Time to Rest

I find it difficult to even sit down to a meal, Father. Resting seems like such a far-fetched notion. I know You want me to find time to rest and spend time with You, but I'm on the go constantly, and I still don't get everything done. Please help me, Lord, to make resting a priority. Amen.

Cast thy burden upon the LORD,
and he shall sustain thee: he shall never
suffer the righteous to be moved.
PSALM 55:22

Showing That
I Love God

How do I show that I love You, God? It must be more than merely a phrase I use in prayer. The way I show it is to keep Your commandments. I need Your strength for this. I fail every day. Renew my desire to live according to Your principles. They are not suggestions. They are commands. Honoring them will cause me to see You at work in my life. I love You, Lord. Amen.

He that hath my commandments, and keepeth them, he it is that loveth me: and he that loveth me shall be loved of my Father, and I will love him, and will manifest myself to him.
JOHN 14:21

Amazing Grace

Lord, I get so caught up in trying to do good works sometimes. I need to remember that I am saved by grace. You are pleased with me simply because I believe in Your Son, Jesus, and I have accepted Him as my Savior. You do not bless me or withhold good gifts based on my performance. Remind me of Your amazing grace, and make me gracious with others. In Jesus' name I pray. Amen.

*For by grace are ye saved through faith;
and that not of yourselves: it is the gift of God:
not of works, lest any man should boast.*
EPHESIANS 2:8–9

Harmful Relationships

Lord, I generally think of relationships as being between people, and I fail to remember that my relationship to things can seriously affect how I react to people. For instance, sometimes I get so involved in a television show that I fail to give needed attention to my family. Forgive me, Father. Be in charge of my relationships. Amen.

---

*And beside this, giving all diligence,
add to your faith virtue; and to virtue
knowledge; and to knowledge temperance;
and to temperance patience; and to patience
godliness; and to godliness brotherly kindness;
and to brotherly kindness charity.*

2 PETER 1:5–7

Steward of Grace

Thank You for the gifts You have given me, Lord. I look around at the other believers in my life. We are all gifted in different ways. Help me to be a good steward of the gifts You have entrusted me with in this life. Instead of looking out for myself, may I have opportunities to use my abilities to minister to others. I understand that it is in doing so that I honor You. Amen.

As every man hath received the gift, even so minister the same one to another, as good stewards of the manifold grace of God.
1 PETER 4:10

An Heir to the King

Heavenly Father, thank You for adopting me as an heir to the King of kings! You provided a way for me to come before You, holy God. Christ carried my sin as His burden. It was nailed to the cross and has been forgiven forever, once and for all. Thank You for the abundant life that is mine because I am Yours. I praise You for viewing me through a lens called grace. Amen.

That being justified by his grace, we should be made heirs according to the hope of eternal life.
TITUS 3:7

Hope for the Future

Lord, I can't see the future. I see only one piece of the puzzle at a time, but You see the finished product. As I go through this day, I will not fear, because You are in control. When things seem hopeless, there is hope. My hope is in a sovereign God who says He knows the plans He has for me. I am counting on You to see me through. Amen.

For I know the thoughts that I think toward you, saith the LORD, thoughts of peace, and not of evil, to give you an expected end.
JEREMIAH 29:11

Loving My Enemies

Lord, some of Your commands are easy to understand, such as taking care of widows and orphans. But some of them go against human nature. It's easier to show mercy to those we love, but You tell us to love our enemies. You command us to love those who are hard to love. Give me a love for the unlovable, Father. I want to have a heart that pleases You. Amen.

For if ye love them which love you, what reward have ye? do not even the publicans the same? And if ye salute your brethren only, what do ye more than others? do not even the publicans so?
MATTHEW 5:46–47

All I Need

Heavenly Father, You are a God of hope, joy, and great love. I don't need signs or wonders. I often wait for people or situations to turn from hopeless to hopeful. But my hope is in You. I need not wait for anything else or look for some other source. I quiet myself before You this morning and ask that You renew the hope within my heart. Thank You, Father. Amen.

And now, Lord, what wait I
for? my hope is in thee.
PSALM 39:7

The Best Relationship

Dear Jesus, I've known many people in my life. I've enjoyed many good relationships and tried to avoid the bad. One thing is certain, though. My relationship with You is the most important. I'm so glad You have time for me and that You want me to fellowship with You. I couldn't ask for a better friend. Amen.

The LORD thy God in the midst of thee is mighty; he will save, he will rejoice over thee with joy; he will rest in his love, he will joy over thee with singing.
ZEPHANIAH 3:17

Love in Deed and Truth

Father, it is easy to say the words "I love you," but it is harder to live them. You want Your children to love their enemies. You tell us to love through action and with truth. These are high callings that require Your Holy Spirit working in us. Use me as a vessel of love today in my little corner of the world. Let me love through my deeds and not just with words. Amen.

My little children, let us not love in word, neither in tongue; but in deed and in truth.
1 JOHN 3:18

Those Left Behind

Father, I'd like to take just a moment to pray for the extended families of missionaries. We often forget that as obedient servants take Your gospel abroad, their relatives are left behind. The separation can be difficult. Ease the loneliness. Bless each family member in a special way. Amen.

*For none of us liveth to himself,
and no man dieth to himself.*
ROMANS 14:7

Bless His Name

Jesus, You alone are worthy of all of my praise. I bless Your name. One day I will worship You with no end, no holding back, and no earthly distraction. I will worship You in heaven forever and ever. . .with the angels and with all of Your people. For today, I go into the world and will choose to bless Your name in the present. Accept my offering of praise. Amen.

And I beheld, and I heard the voice of many angels round about the throne and the beasts and the elders: and the number of them was ten thousand times ten thousand, and thousands of thousands; saying with a loud voice, Worthy is the Lamb that was slain to receive power, and riches, and wisdom, and strength, and honour, and glory, and blessing.
REVELATION 5:11–12

The Beauty of the Lord

May my pursuit of You, Lord, be my "one thing." May I praise You and serve You in this life, which is but training camp for eternity! I look forward to heaven, Father, where I may truly know the depths of Your beauty. I see glimpses of Your beauty in Your creation. One day it will be fully revealed. What a glorious day that will be! Until then, be my "one thing." I love You, Lord. Amen.

One thing have I desired of the LORD, that will I seek after; that I may dwell in the house of the LORD all the days of my life, to behold the beauty of the LORD, and to enquire in his temple.

PSALM 27:4

Only One Master

Father, there are so many things in this world that fight for my affection. It seems there is always a new product or style that the advertisements say I can't live without! It is easy to get caught up in materialism. Guard my heart, Father, and guard even my tongue. Remind me that the word *love* should not be used loosely. I love You, Father. Be Lord of my life, I pray. Amen.

No man can serve two masters: for either he will hate the one, and love the other; or else he will hold to the one, and despise the other. Ye cannot serve God and mammon.
MATTHEW 6:24

Modest Example

So many people think that modesty is only a clothing issue, but You've shown me that it's so much more. It's an attitude akin to humility, and it's what You want from me. Even in this You set the example for me, Jesus. Help me follow the pattern You've given me. Amen.

In like manner also, that women adorn themselves in modest apparel, with shamefacedness and sobriety; not with broided hair, or gold, or pearls, or costly array; but (which becometh women professing godliness) with good works.
1 Timothy 2:9–10

Up from the Grave

Hope is a living, breathing thing. I see that now, Lord. I'd always pictured it as a word. A choice. A lifeless thing. But it's not. It's very much alive, quickening my heart even now. Hope boosts the adrenaline. Hope steadies my breathing. Hope shifts my focus. Hope keeps my feet moving. And this hope is alive in me because of the resurrection of Your Son, Jesus. Amazing! When He rose from the dead, He set in motion a hope that refuses to die. What an awesome, motivational gift, Father. I praise You for this hope. Amen.

Through him you believe in God,
who raised him from the dead and glorified
him, and so your faith and hope are in God.
1 PETER 1:21 NIV

Perfect Holiness

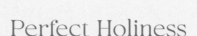

God, when I consider my own inadequacies, I am amazed at Your perfectness. You are truth and justice, holiness and integrity. There is none like You. You are the one and only true God. Other deities disappoint their followers; idols fail. But You never do. Because You are perfect holiness, all Your other attributes are only good. There is no selfishness, vengefulness, or deceitfulness in You, Lord. Thus, I can trust You completely and revel in Your light unafraid. Amen.

"No one is holy like the LORD, for there is none besides You, nor is there any rock like our God."
1 SAMUEL 2:2 NKJV

Peace, Please

Dear Jesus, someone I love dearly is in the hospital. I'm sitting here in the busy waiting room, watching for the doctor, wanting news, and yet dreading to hear it. Others surround me, connected to this place by a person they care about. We're people from every stratum and season of life with one thing in common— knowing someone who is suffering physically. Lord, illness and injury have to obey Your will, and so do the emotions that burden the hearts of those here. Please visit every waiting area and patient's room, and bring the cure that only comes from You—tranquility, mercy, and courage. Amen.

Now the God of peace be with you all.
ROMANS 15:33 NKJV

That Important
First Step

Lord, my neighbors are some of the most rude and inconsiderate people I've ever known. It's hard not to complain about them, but I don't have a right to. They aren't Christians, and I've never witnessed to them. Why would they act differently? Forgive me, Father. I will take them Your Word. Please open their hearts. Amen.

---

*Walk in wisdom toward them that
are without, redeeming the time.*
COLOSSIANS 4:5

Demonstrating Love

God, I have the most demanding boss ever. I need to demonstrate the love of Christ, but it can be challenging when my superior is, at times, so hard to please. Give me courage, Lord, to rise above my emotions. Help me to pray for my boss as the Bible tells me to and to serve as though it is an assignment from You. For You, Lord, are my true superior. Bless my boss today, God, and show Your love to him through me. Amen.

Whatever you do, work at it with all your heart, as working for the Lord, not for human masters.
COLOSSIANS 3:23 NIV

Technology

Dear God, the internet is a marvelous tool! Thank You for giving humankind the ability to invent it. But the internet also has a great potential for evil. I ask You to protect my family from online predators, from sexual content, from sites that would have a negative influence on our relationship with You. Help me to be prudent in my use of the web. Like any other means of communication, it can be used wrongly. But, with Your help, it can be an instrument for good in our home. Amen.

I will set nothing wicked before my eyes.
PSALM 101:3 NKJV

A Sense of Purpose

Father, I'm in a rut. I like some familiarity, but this monotony is wearing away at my sense of purpose. I know there are parts of our lives that are not particularly glamorous, fulfilling, or significant (at least, on the surface). Yet living without passion or purpose isn't what You had in mind for us. Show me, Lord, how to find meaning in my everyday life. Open up to my eyes the subtle nuances of joy folded into life's mundane hours. I put my longings into Your hands. Amen.

In Him also we have obtained an inheritance, being predestined according to the purpose of Him who works all things according to the counsel of His will.
EPHESIANS 1:11 NKJV

One Nation under God

Dear God, I am so weary of the bickering in our nation. It disturbs me to see people attempting to remove You from schools, courtrooms, and anywhere else they think of. They distort history and deny that this nation was founded with You as her leader. Heal us, Lord. Help us return to You! Amen.

I am the light of the world: he that followeth me shall not walk in darkness, but shall have the light of life.
JOHN 8:12

Help with Priorities

Dear God, I need help with my priorities. It is so easy for them to get out of whack. Show me the things I've let creep to the top that don't belong there. Point out to me those areas where I need to put more emphasis and commitment. Lord, let me remember that people are worth more than possessions and pursuits. Let my unseen checklist of priorities reflect that. Amen.

"For wherever your treasure is, you may be certain that your heart will be there too!"
MATTHEW 6:21 PHILLIPS

Don't Worry!

Dear Lord, Your Word tells me it is wrong to worry. I try to tell myself that it's only concern, but actually, that's putting a nice spin on the issue. Older women used to say that females are just born worriers. I guess there's some truth to that, maybe because we're so invested in relationships, and most of our worrying is about those we love and care for. Still, You know worry isn't good for us and it doesn't accomplish anything. So, today, help me not to worry, but to turn all my "concerns" over to You.

Don't worry over anything whatever;
tell God every detail of your needs in earnest
and thankful prayer, and the peace of God
which transcends human understanding,
will keep constant guard over your hearts
and minds as they rest in Christ Jesus.
PHILIPPIANS 4:6–7 PHILLIPS

Think on Pure Things

There's just not much in today's society that encourages purity, but Your Word certainly demonstrates the importance of focusing our attention on things that are pure. From experience, I have learned that life is more satisfying when it's geared toward pleasing You rather than the flesh, and I thank You for these lessons. Amen.

Ye shall walk after the LORD your God, and fear him, and keep his commandments, and obey his voice, and ye shall serve him, and cleave unto him.

DEUTERONOMY 13:4

Confidante

Dear God, the Bible tells older women to mentor younger women. That's an element missing from my life. Although my mom did a great job of passing along the life lessons she'd learned, and we have a good relationship, I still need the insight and affirmation of an older woman. Lord, I need a trusted confidante, one who will help me succeed. I ask You to send someone like that my way in fulfillment of Your Word. And let me fill that role myself someday when I have the required résumé. Amen.

May [the aged women] teach the young women to be sober, to love their husbands, to love their children.
TITUS 2:4

Gentle Peace

Thank You, Lord, for this opportunity to bask in the peace that You offer. As I sit here in the woods, listening to the creek gently bubbling over the stones, I am reminded how Your presence in my life soothes even in the midst of chaos. I'm glad I have Your peace! Amen.

The Lord bless thee, and keep thee: the Lord make his face shine upon thee, and be gracious unto thee: the Lord lift up his countenance upon thee, and give thee peace.
NUMBERS 6:24–26

Life's Security System

Father, I deal with a phobia. It isn't anything life threatening, but it's embarrassing. I haven't told anyone, and I'm hoping I never have to. But I ask You now to help me; I don't want my phobia to keep me from living the life You've planned for me. Help me to bring this fear to You; show me that You are in control, that You are the security system in my life. I ask this in Jesus' name. Amen.

For God has not given us a spirit of fear, but a spirit of power and love and a sound mind.
2 TIMOTHY 1:7 PHILLIPS

Instant Gratification

Dear Lord, so many things are instantaneous in my world. From fast food to instant credit, we can satisfy our penchant for immediate gratification at every juncture. But I have to keep reminding myself that You often work by process. When it comes to the work You're doing in me, You use the steady maturing of Your Word within me to make me more like Jesus. You, the master gardener, water the seeds, prune the unnecessary limbs, and watch over me carefully as the fruit of my life continues to ripen. Instead of being impatient, I aim to revel in Your timely and tender loving care. Amen.

But grow in grace, and in the knowledge of our Lord and Saviour Jesus Christ.
2 PETER 3:18

Letting Go of Bitterness

Bitterness is like cancer, God. It grows and takes over, squeezing out life. I don't want to be marked or consumed by bitterness. Let me not hold to the injustices I've experienced. Help me accept Your healing touch and let go of the beginnings of bitterness in my soul. As Joseph noted in the Old Testament, You can turn things meant for evil into good. Please do that in my life. In Christ's name, amen.

Let all bitterness, wrath, anger, clamor, and evil speaking be put away from you, with all malice.
EPHESIANS 4:31 NKJV

For Each New Day

Every day there is something I can offer
You praise for, dear God! To begin with, we
have the promise of a fresh start—a new
opportunity to serve You. Throughout the
day You show Your majesty in a multitude of
ways. You are an awesome God! Amen.

And of his fulness have all we
received, and grace for grace.
JOHN 1:16

Today!

Father in heaven, I have a tendency to try to live a week or month at a time. It's difficult for me to limit myself to one day, one hour, one minute. But that's how You want me to live. You know that projecting into the future causes me to wonder and worry about things that haven't happened yet. You also know that I can't be any good to anyone if my head is in the clouds, thinking about the future. So help me live in today—it's all I have at the moment. Amen.

---

*"Does He not see my ways,
and count all my steps?"*

JOB 31:4 NKJV

Claim Peace

Father, peace is an elusive emotion. So many people talk about peace, but few can claim it. You promised to give us Your peace, a calm assurance that You are present and sovereign in all our ways. I want more of this peace every day. Although there are many upsetting things in my world, Your peace will help me cope with them all. Amid Your peace, I am neither troubled nor afraid, merely allowing myself to bask in Your presence. Amen.

"Peace I leave with you,
My peace I give to you."
JOHN 14:27 NKJV

New Compassions

I really didn't want to get up this morning, Father. My blankets seemed like good protection from the cares of the day. But when I saw the glorious sunrise and heard the cheerful, singing birds, I was reminded that Your compassions are new every morning. I knew everything would be fine. Thank You for Your faithfulness.

Sing unto the LORD, bless his name;
shew forth his salvation from day to day.
PSALM 96:2

From the Mountain

Lord, it feels good to be alive! When I got out of bed this morning, I had this wonderful sense of well-being. Some days I awaken with something negative on my mind, some trouble on the horizon, or some ache in my body. But today I feel great in mind, spirit, and body. This road of life has both mountains and valleys. But right now, I'm going to enjoy the mountain— the brightness, the beauty, and the refreshing that will help me face any challenge that comes my way today or tomorrow. I love You, Lord. Thank You for good surprises!

Oh, give thanks to the LORD, for He is good! For His mercy endures forever.
PSALM 107:1 NKJV

When I'm Not Prepared

Father God, I've put myself in a bind because I procrastinated. I knew this was looming ahead of me, but I wanted to do other things first. Or, at least, I wanted to leave the task until the right time. But now, there is no more time, and I'm not prepared. Please help me, Lord, working all things to my good. Amen.

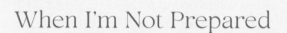

Make the most of every opportunity.
EPHESIANS 5:16 NLT

He's in Control

Thank You, Lord, that You have a perfect plan for my life. I know I don't always understand it, but You know what's best, and everything that happens is for a reason—that You might be glorified. I'm so glad that You are in control and that I need not worry. Amen.

There are many devices in a man's heart; nevertheless the counsel of the LORD, that shall stand.

PROVERBS 19:21

Scripture Index

OLD TESTAMENT

NEW TESTAMENT

Strengthen Your Faith by Growing Your Prayer Life

180 Prayers for a Peaceful Spirit
This devotional prayer title packs a powerful dose of inspiration into just-right-sized readings to help you experience the peace of Christ. Each prayer, written specifically for your devotional quiet time, will meet you right where you are—and is complemented by a relevant scripture and question for further thought.

Flexible Casebound /
978-1-63609-895-1

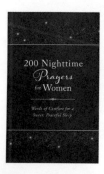

200 Nighttime Prayers for Women
These 200 comforting prayers—written just for you—will soothe your tired soul and usher in peaceful relaxation at bedtime. Each prayer is the perfect way for you to draw closer to the rest giver and hand all of the worries and cares of your day over to Him.

Hardback / 978-1-64352-003-2